CROSS-STITCH WITH CATTITUDE

20 pawsome designs

EMMA CONGDON

DAVID & CHARLES

www.davidandcharles.com

CONTENTS

Welcome to
Cross Stitch with Cattitude

- the cross stitch equivalent of a bowl
of cream for owners and admirers of
feisty felines everywhere - inspired by
my own beloved and infuriating cats,
past and present.

If you have a well behaved, loving and
cooperative cat that causes zero bother
please proceed no further. This book is
not for you. If however, you have a demon
that screams for food at four o'clock in
the morning, won't let you use the toilet
alone, and gets stuck in furniture, this
might be the book you've been waiting for.

Proceed with caution... **and kibble.**

TOOLS AND MATERIALS

FABRIC

When it comes to fabric there are so many options, but Aida is a great choice. The pre-woven holes make stitching a breeze. I'm all about enjoyment when it comes to stitching and, as much as I appreciate the neatness of Jobelan or Hardanger, I find Aida much easier to work with (easier than cats anyway).

Throughout this book I have recommended specific fabrics to use for each piece. These are chosen to work best with the colours but, of course, substitutions can always be made to suit your own style and material choices. Here's a simple breakdown of the fabric types you might want to consider:

SUSTAINABILITY

Cotton, although a natural fabric, does use a lot of water and pesticides to produce, and contributes to environmental pollution when not farmed in an organic way. I always try to waste as little of it as possible when working with it.

Organic cotton is considerably better for the environment but is not widely available for cross stitching at this present moment (though hopefully it will be in the future).

Linen, when farmed correctly, has a much lower carbon footprint than cotton so makes an excellent choice if you want to be a little bit more conscious about the impact of your materials.

Choose your cat litter brand wisely. What is its environmental impact? Will you have to throw the whole bag away if it doesn't meet your cat's exacting requirements?

Aida is a cotton fabric, woven specifically for cross stitch. It has a natural mesh that helps guide the stitcher, and enough stiffness that for smaller projects an embroidery hoop isn't always required.

Fiddler's cloth is similar to Aida but slightly irregular, producing a rustic, aged look, which is good if you want something a little less perfect.

Hardanger is made of 100% cotton at 22-count weave. Usually used for 'Hardanger embroidery', it also works for cross stitch. Its denser weave can make it trickier to work, but the results can be well worth it.

Linen has a finer weave than Aida, and is usually stitched over two threads. It offers a more traditional look. Working with linen can also be a challenge, so you might want to consider 'linen Aida', which combines the qualities of both.

Jobelan is soft with a slight sheen. It's stitched over two threads, but is more resistant to wrinkles than linen. Easy to wash, it is ideal for larger projects, such as tablecloths.

The term **evenweave** applies to all fabric that is 'evenly woven'. The fabric will have the same number of threads per inch, horizontally and vertically. 28-count evenweave is stitched over two threads of fabric, so it is the same as 14-count Aida.

THREAD

Thread is the paint of the stitching world and offers endless creative possibilities. For counted cross stitch it's super simple to use and the worst that can happen is that it can knot (as long as you keep it out of reach of You Know Who). I recommend working with two strands for whole stitches (so dividing the original thread into three sets of two strands) and then working with lengths of around 30–50cm (12–20in), adjusting them on your needle to get started. For backstitch use a single strand.

In this book I have used DMC stranded cotton (floss), but there are many alternatives available and the conversion chart at the end of this book will help you to get the closest colour matches.

Using thread from well known brands is best from an environmental standpoint, as their manufacture is likely to be less polluting than cheaper flosses. Both DMC and Anchor threads are produced in accordance with Oeko-Tex® Standard 100, ensuring flosses are free from banned azo dyes, as well as carcinogenic and allergenic dyestuffs.

SCISSORS

Good embroidery scissors are sharp and fine-pointed for cleanly cutting thread, and for snipping off loose ends. To keep them sharp, never use them to cut paper or fabric, or to open pouches of delicious cat food, however urgently it is required. Instead you will need a separate pair of fabric scissors for cutting your Aida or linen.

NEEDLES

You can get by with ones that are too big or too small, but using a good embroidery needle that is the right size for the fabric will make stitching much easier. Tapestry needles are best for cross stitch because they have a rounded point so will not snag the fabric. However, for your safety and that of your cat, always be careful with where they are left (please never, ever, cross stitch in bed!). A magnetic needle minder is a good place to 'park' your needle when it's not in use.

FRAMES AND HOOPS

Frames keep your fabric taut while working, can save you a huge amount of time and also ensure that your stitching is even. I like to keep it simple and use a bamboo hoop (which is also much better than a plastic one from an environmental standpoint) but there are many varieties available, including some really fancy ones that you don't even have to hold! Try out a few different models if you're unsure.

KIBBLE

To ensure a reasonable length of uninterrupted sewing time, always check that bowls are freshly topped up. Kibble requirements may vary day to day. Your cats will let you know.

"My humans (aka the staff) are marginally more tOLeraBle than your average homo sapiens, but that's only because they make my life so easy with their ENDless attempts to win me over. Keep those treats coming and perhaps I won't LeAVE."

X

need to know

Stitch count: 103 x 103

Stitched size (on 16-count Aida): 16.5 x 16.5cm (6½ x 6½in)

Stitch with two strands for cross stitch.

Essential supplies

- 1 skein of each DMC stranded cotton (floss) listed in the chart key

- 16-count Aida in Antique White, at least 37 x 37cm (14½ x 14½in)

- 20.5cm (8in) diameter bamboo embroidery hoop for framing

MODEL STITCHED BY SHARON ATKINSON

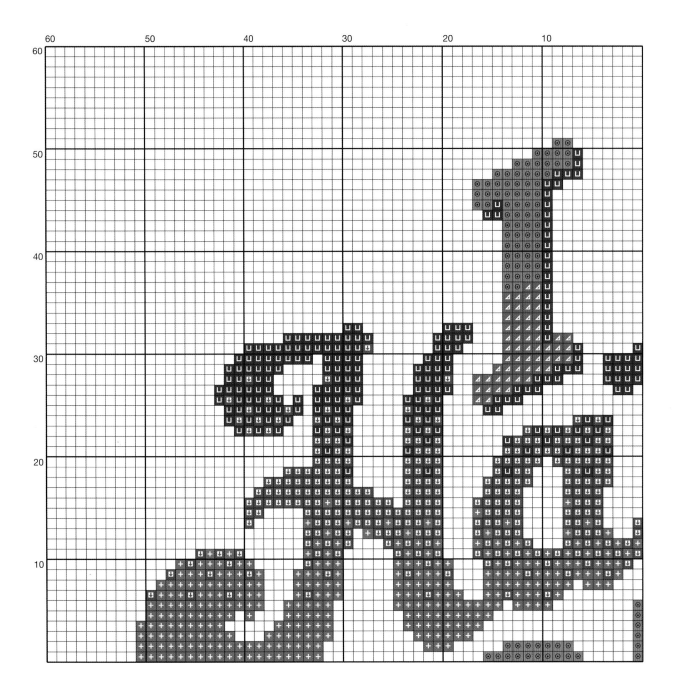

THREAD KEY

- **Z** 155
- **□** 310
- **◄** 351
- **◉** 603
- **↓** 831
- **◑** 3865
- **◼** 165
- **◪** 333
- **◢** 602
- **U** 829
- **+** 832

11

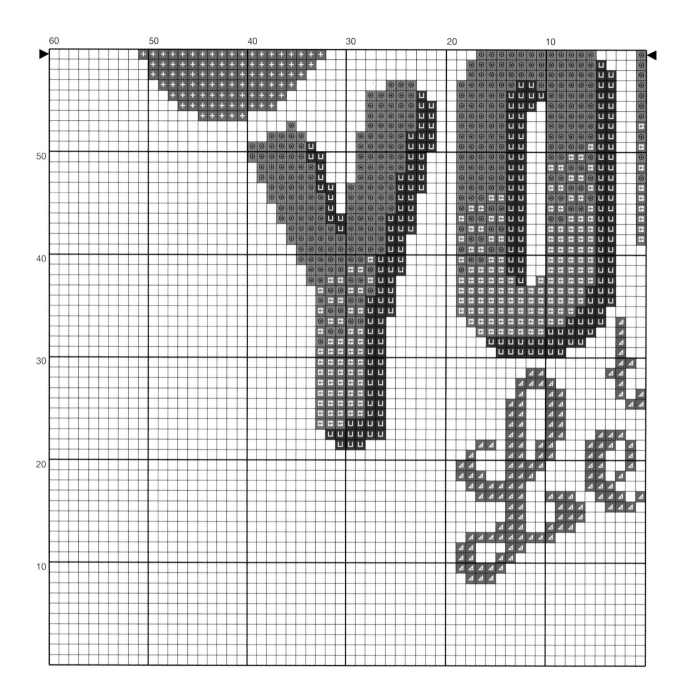

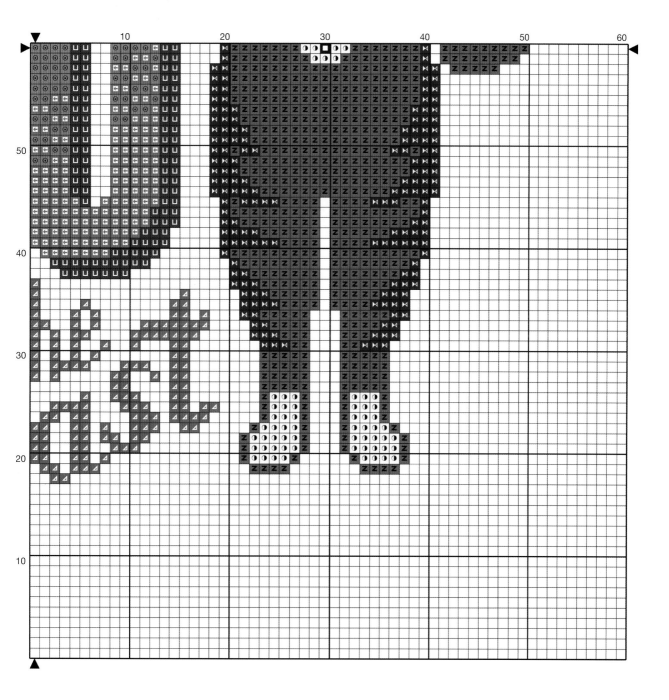

THREAD KEY

- **Z** 155
- **□** 310
- **←** 351
- **◉** 603
- **↓** 831
- **◐** 3865
- **■** 165
- **⋈** 333
- **◢** 602
- **⊔** 829
- **✛** 832

"**IMAGINE** thinking extra terrestrials would be remotely interested in **humans!** It's us they're really here for. They have excellent **kibble,** and they call us by our true names rather than hairball-inducing human nonsense, like '**Pussykins**'..."

x

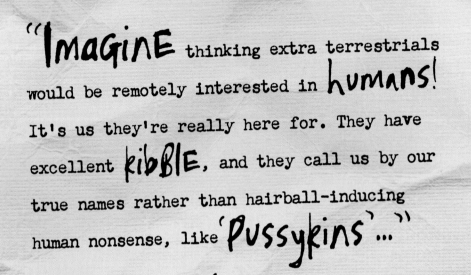

Need to know

Stitch count: 112 x 110

Stitched size (on 16-count Aida): 18 x 17.5cm (7⅛ x 6⅞in)

Stitch with two strands for cross stitch.

Essential supplies

• 1 skein of each DMC stranded cotton (floss) listed in the chart key

• 16-count Aida in Black, at least 38 x 38cm (15 x 15in)

MODEL STITCHED BY ELEANOR COOPER

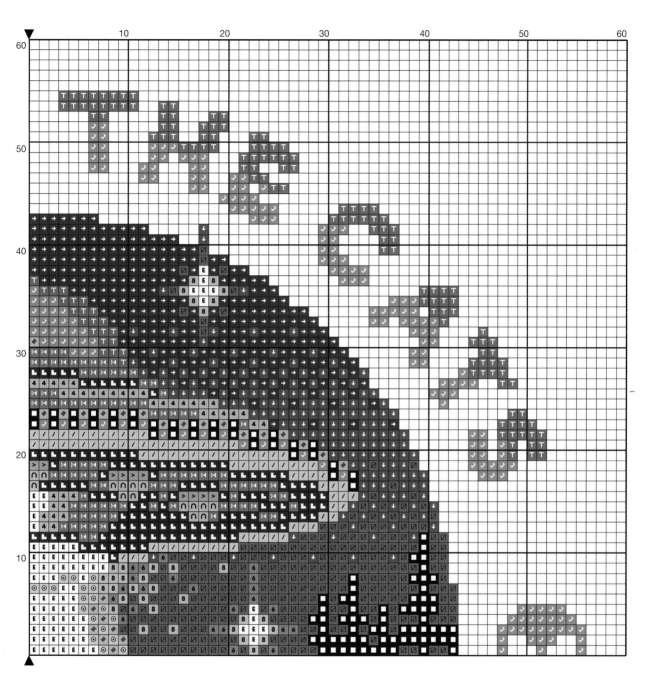

ThREAd KEy

/	1	6	603	4	2	8	605
⋈	4	✓	704	⊙	14	>	741
❋	16	←	904	↓	33	T	906
☐	310	▨	3607	◿	319	→	3837
◳	413	E	Blanc	∩	444		

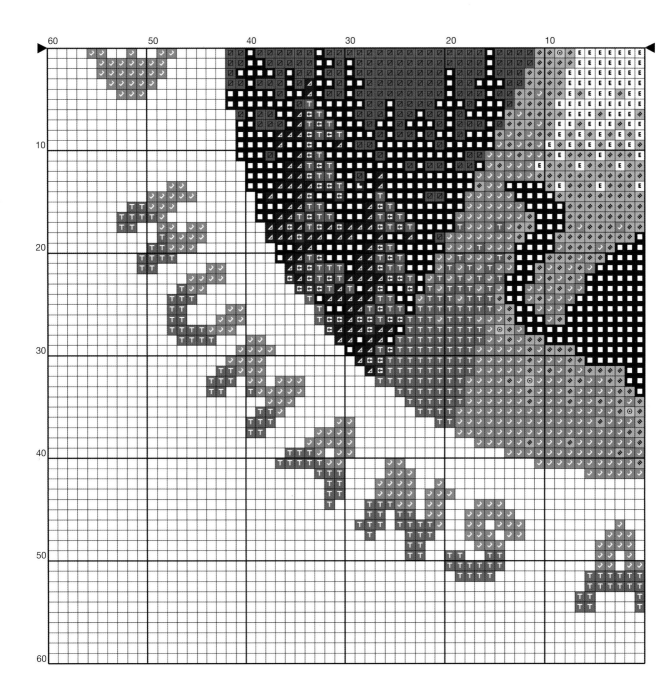

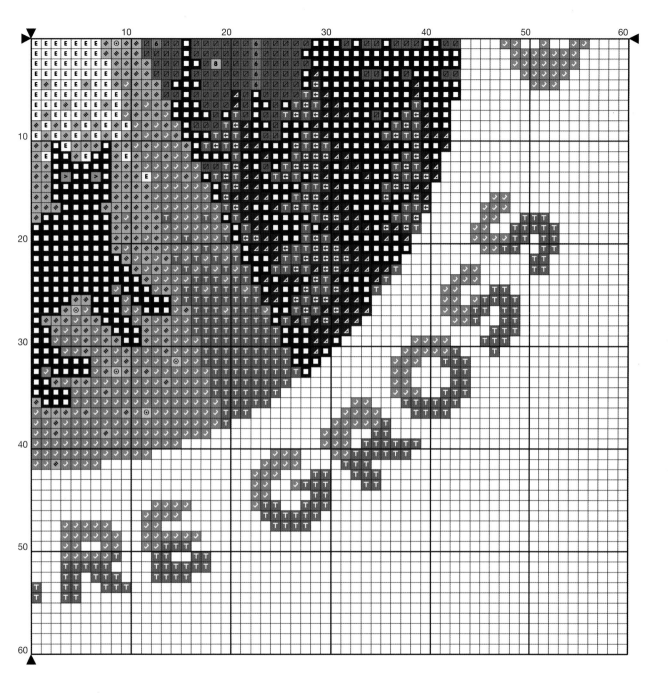

THREAD KEY

Symbol	Color	Symbol	Color	Symbol	Color	Symbol	Color
/	1	6	603	4	2	8	605
⊠	4	✔	704	⊙	14	>	741
◈	16	←	904	↓	33	T	906
□	310	⧄	3607	◢	319	→	3837
⌐	413	E	Blanc	∩	444		

"*Feline* rules dictate that all human requests be **ignored**. The carpet, not the wipe-able kitchen floor, is the only acceptable place to regurgitate a **hairball**. And don't assume we always want to **poo** in a box..."

x

need to know

Stitch count: 58 x 110

Stitched size (on 18-count Aida):
8.5 x 15.5cm (33/8 x 6⅛in)

Stitch with two strands for cross stitch.

Essential supplies

- 1 skein of each DMC stranded cotton (floss) listed in the chart key

- 18-count Aida in Baby Pink, at least 28 x 35.5cm (11 x 14in)

MODEL STITCHED BY ELEANOR COOPER

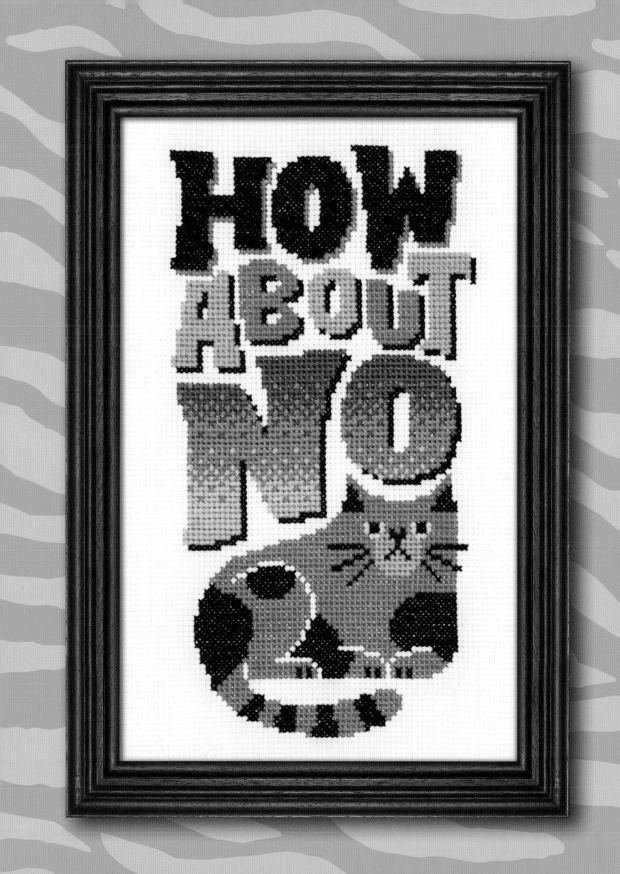

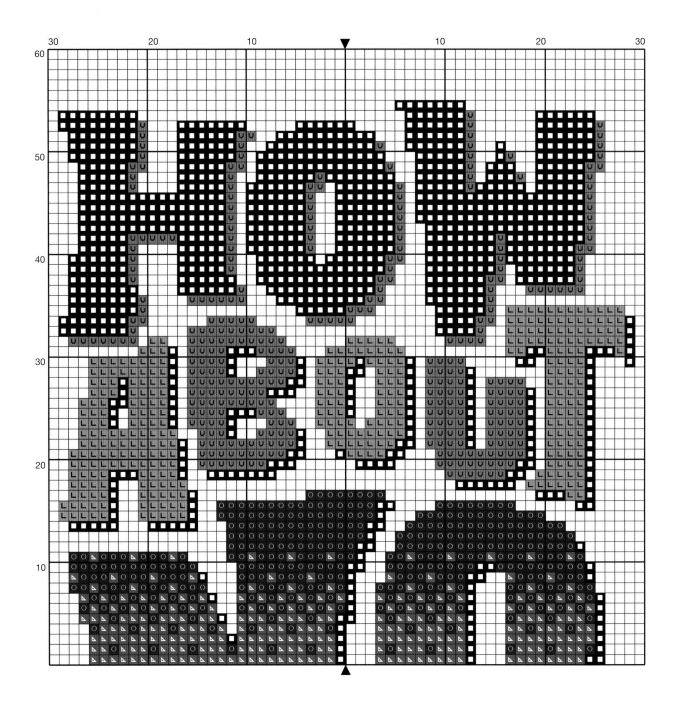

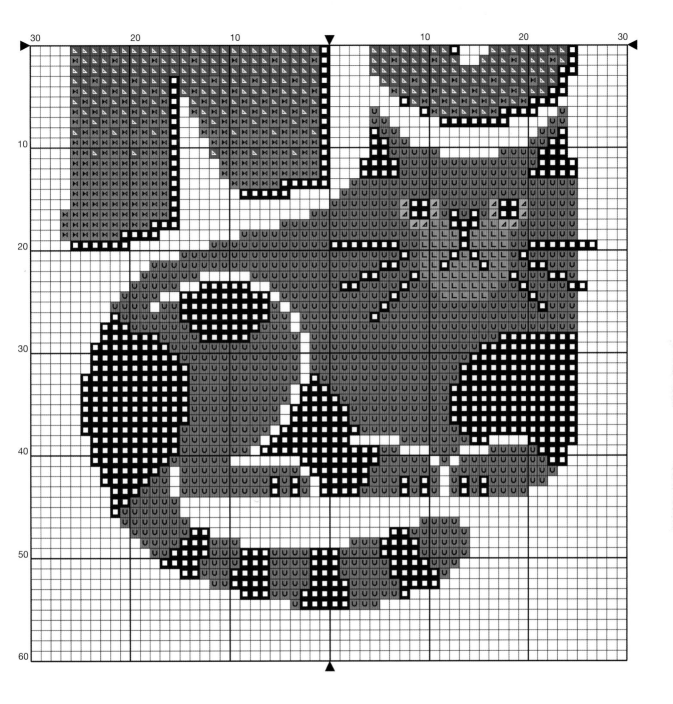

THREAD KEY

- ☐ 310
- Ⓞ 3847
- U 602
- L 603
- ✕ 959
- ◣ 3812
- ◢ 16

"**Cat hair** is basically a **(FABulous)** uniform cat owners use to identify each other. We leave it **EVERYWHERE** to remind you we're always close by. You'll find it in the most curious places... including your dinner. **Bon appetit!**"

x

Need to know

Stitch count: 86 x 108

Stitched size (on 14-count Aida): 16 x 19.5cm (6⅜ x 7¾in)

Stitch with three strands for cross stitch, and one strand for backstitch.

Essential supplies

• 1 skein of each DMC stranded cotton (floss) listed in the chart key

• 14-count Aida in Black, at least 37 x 39.5cm (14½ x 15½in)

MODEL STITCHED BY GLENDA DICKSON

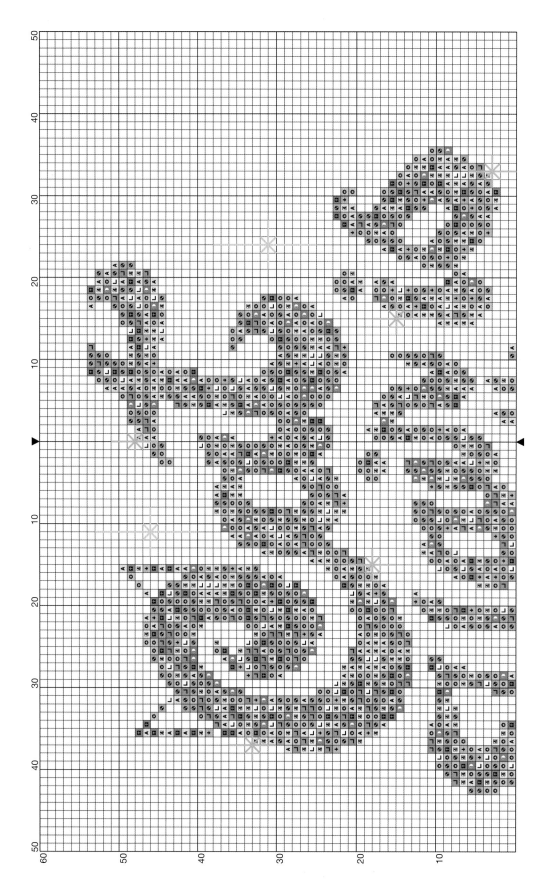

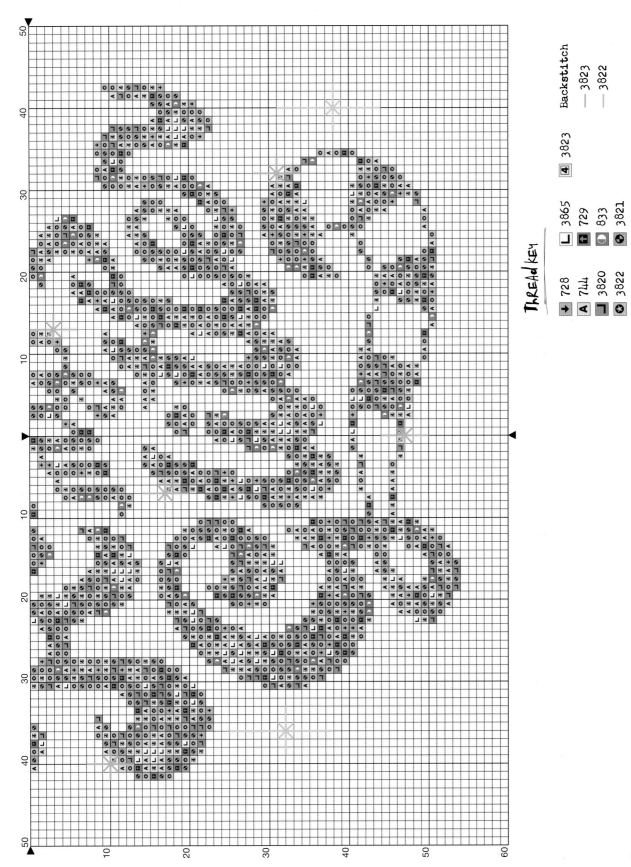

THREAD KEY

→ 728	L 3865	4 3823	Backstitch
A 744	← 729		— 3823
⌐ 3820	⬤ 833		— 3822
✿ 3822	✦ 3821		

27

"**Some** humans think we're all the same. What a **Cheek!** We're as individual as they are, **but** obviously just a lot more **attractive.**"

x

need to know

Stitch count: 122 x 158

Stitched size (on 14-count Aida):
22 x 28.5cm (8⅝ x 11¼in)

Stitch with two strands for cross stitch, and one strand for backstitch.

Essential supplies

• 1 skein of each DMC stranded cotton (floss) listed in the chart key - if a colour requires more than one skein the number needed is indicated in brackets after the colour

• 14-count Aida in White, at least 42 x 49.5cm (16½ x 19½in)

MODEL STITCHED BY ELEANOR COOPER

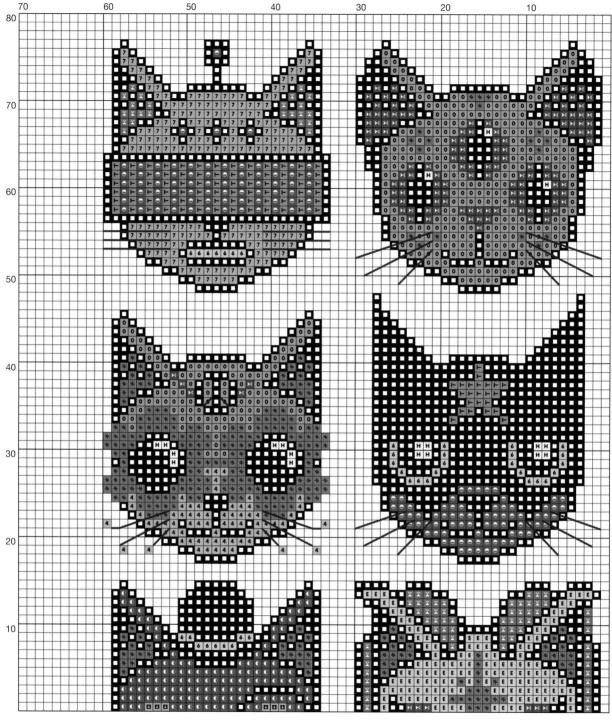

ThREAd KEY

155	437	742	E 963	3806	H Blanc	310 (4)	721	921	3761	3845
6 307	606	911	977	3826	7 E168	604	813	964	0 3819

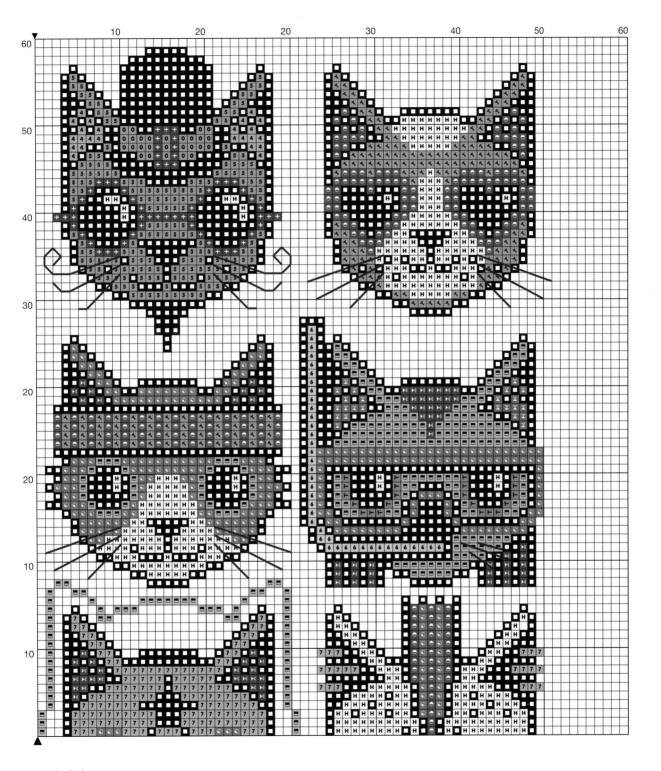

Backstitch

— 310

— 3806

THREAD KEY

Symbol	Color
⋈ 155	
5 437	
4 742	
E 963	
⬥ 3806	
H Blanc	
☐ 310 (4)	
721	
◑ 921	
▬ 3761	
⊠ 3845	
6 307	
⬬ 606	
⋈ 911	
┝ 977	
✚ 3826	
7 E168	
⬦ 604	
◪ 813	
⬆ 964	
0 3819	

Backstitch

— 310

— 3806

"There's no such thing as a **CRAZY** cat lady – anyone who prefers us over humans is making a logical and **SEnSiBLe** choice. These people sometimes begin their **CAT** journey with just one of us, but it's **NEVER** long before they want more."

X

need to know

Stitch count: 114 x 115

Stitched size (on 16-count Aida): 18 x 18.5cm (7⅛ x 7¼in)

Stitch with two strands for cross stitch, and one strand for backstitch.

Essential supplies

- 1 skein of each DMC stranded cotton (floss) listed in the chart key

- 16-count Aida in Navy, at least 38 x 38cm (15 x 15in)

- 20.5cm (8in) diameter bamboo embroidery hoop for framing

MODEL STITCHED BY SHARON ATKINSON

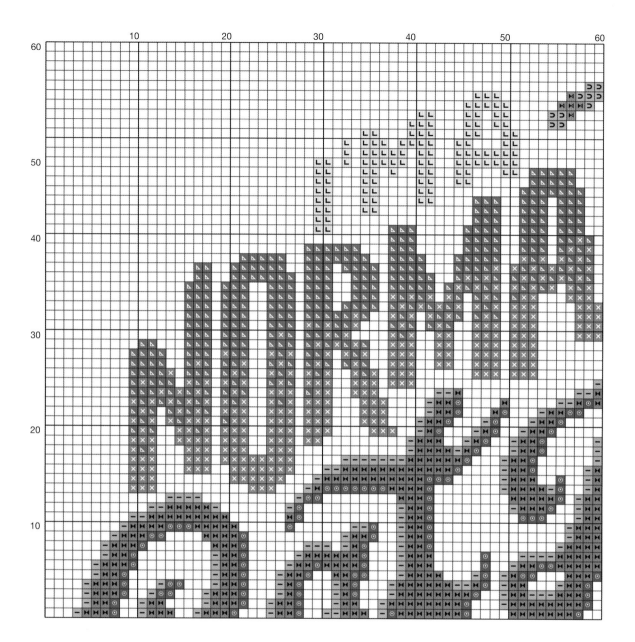

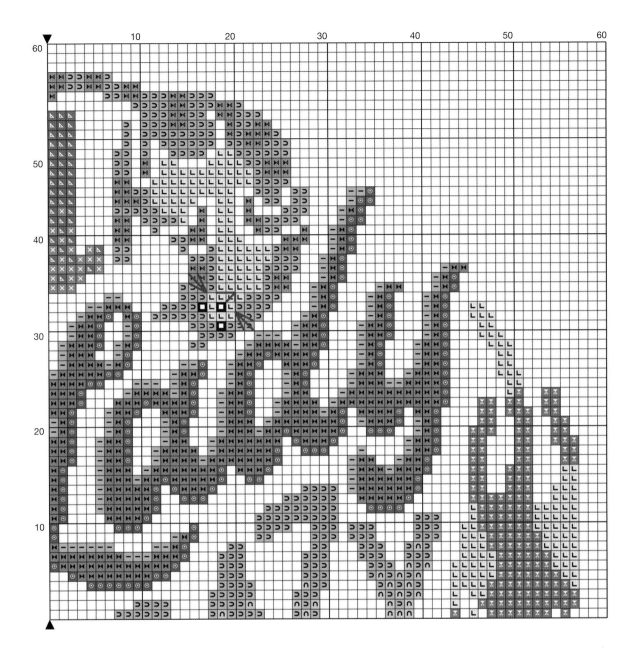

THREAD KEY

Symbol	Color	Symbol	Color	Symbol	Color	Symbol	Color
∩	19	⋈	959	•	355	⊙	3812
⊠	351	⋈	3608	✕	704		
⌐	605	⊃	3825	◣	912		
L	818	☐	310	—	964		

Backstitch
— 310

THREAD KEY

Symbol	Color	Symbol	Color	Symbol	Color	Symbol	Color
∩	19	⋈	959	•	355	⊙	3812
⊠	351	⋈	3608	✕	704		
Γ	605	⊃	3825	◥	912		
L	818	□	310	–	964		

Backstitch
— 310

" I know I'm **Pretty**, that's obvious. I mean... just **Look** at me. What I don't know is why the **kibble** bowl is **empty** again. Can someone look into this please? "

x

need to know

Stitch count: 89 x 122

Stitched size (on 16-count Aida): 14.5 x 19cm (5¾ x 7½in)

Stitch with two strands for cross stitch, and one strand for backstitch.

Essential supplies

- 1 skein of each DMC stranded cotton (floss) listed in the chart key. If a colour requires more than one skein the number needed is indicated in brackets after the colour

- 16-count Aida in Antique White, at least 34 x 39.5cm (13⅜ x 15½in)

MODEL STITCHED BY ELEANOR COOPER

"Sometimes I'm **AbsoLutely**
not in the mood... for any of it.
Leave me **CURLED** up in a corner
for a bit and I'll eventually get
OVER it. Until then..."

x

need to know

Stitch count: 87 x 121

Stitched size (on 16-count Aida):
14 x 19cm (5½ x 7½in)

Stitch with two strands for
cross stitch.

Essential supplies

- 1 skein of each DMC stranded
  cotton (floss) listed in the chart
  key. If a colour requires more
  than one skein the number needed
  is indicated in brackets after
  the colour

- 16-count Aida in Misty Blue, at
  least 34 x 39.5cm (13⅜ x 15½in)

MODEL STITCHED BY GLENDA DICKSON

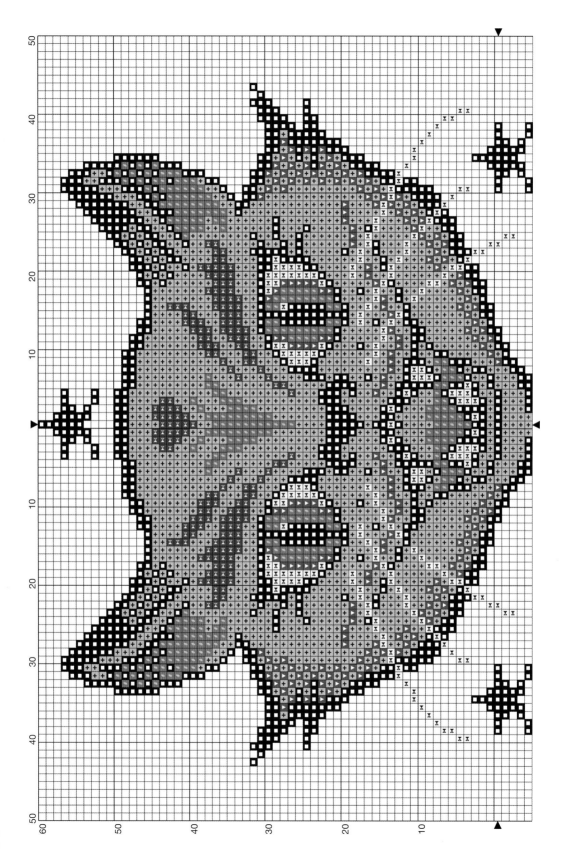

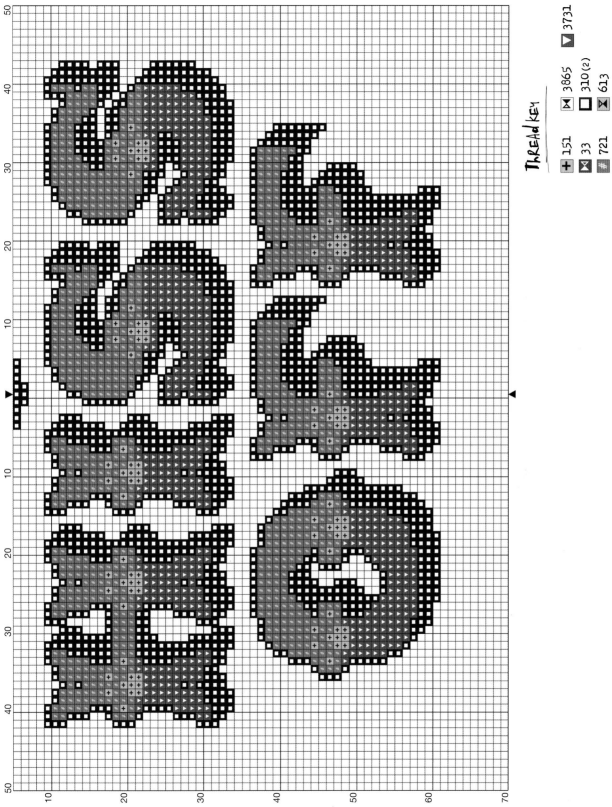

THREAD KEY

+ 151	3865	3731
33	310 (2)	
# 721	613	

" We are the most **SARCASTIC** beings on earth, so we sometimes have to **SLEEP** to stop you being overwhelmed by our **SUPERIOR** wit."

X

need to know

Stitch count: 85 x 121

Stitched size (on 14-count Aida): 15.5 x 22cm (6⅛ x 8⅝in)

Stitch with two strands for cross stitch, and one strand for backstitch.

Essential supplies

- 1 skein of each DMC stranded cotton (floss) listed in the chart key

- 14-count Aida or 28-count evenweave in Ivory, at least 35.5 x 42cm (14 x 16½in)

MODEL STITCHED BY HAYLEY WELLOCK

THREAD KEY

	161		351
◻	161	▨	351
⊠	676	Ⓝ	783
Ⓞ	932	▶	3733
Ⓒ	3752		3752

Backstitch
— 161

"The human **LOVES** hanging out with me in front of the TV. They never offer me wine though, which I'm deeply **OFFENDED** by. **I Loved** a good merlot in a former life. I often eat the **snacks** when they've gone."

x

need to know

Stitch count: 80 x 121

Stitched size (on 14-count Aida): 14.5 x 22cm (5¾ x 8⅝in)

Stitch with two strands for cross stitch, and one strand for backstitch.

Essential supplies

- 1 skein of each DMC stranded cotton (floss) listed in the chart key. If a colour requires more than one skein the number needed is indicated in brackets after the colour

- 14-count Aida in White, at least 34 x 42cm (13⅜ x 16½in)

MODEL STITCHED BY GLENDA DICKSON

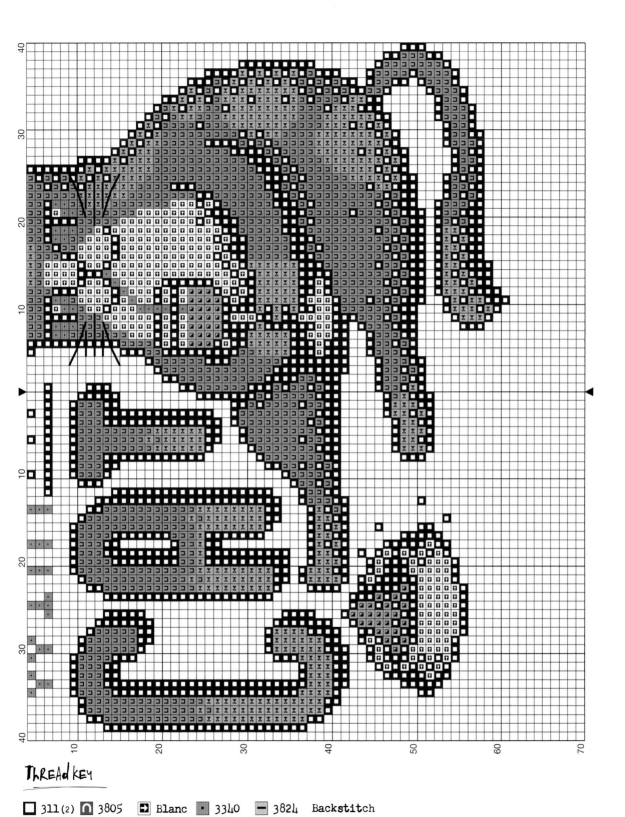

ThREAd KEy

□ 311(2)	⌒ 3805	→ Blanc	▨ 3340	▬ 3824	Backstitch
⊔ 996	◣ 3821	▨ 826	⋈ 3806		▬ 832

"As your **BOSS** it is only correct that I keep a keen **EYE** on your performance. I'll appear in video calls, sporadically and without **WARNING**, and will edit written work when access to the **KEYBOARD** allows."

X

need to know

Stitch count: 85 x 120

Stitched size (on 28-count evenweave): 15.5 x 22cm (6⅛ x 8⅝in)

Stitch with two strands for cross stitch.

Essential supplies

- 1 skein of each DMC stranded cotton (floss) listed in the chart key. If a colour requires more than one skein the number needed is indicated in brackets after the colour

- 28-count evenweave in White, at least 35.5 x 42cm (14 x 16½in)

- 23cm (9in) diameter bamboo embroidery hoop for framing

MODEL STITCHED BY SHARON ATKINSON

THREAD KEY

Symbol	Color	Symbol	Color
X 17		◇ 3838(2)	○ 3812
□ 310		◢ 301	⊙ 3865
∩ 894		○ 797	
▷ 3766		✕ 3340	

"We are so very, very **hungry**, and look, the bowl is empty. Your **human** memory is feeble and unreliable. We have not been **Fed**. The merest suggestion that we are lying is an **insult**. One which can **only** be remedied with food."

X

Need to know

Stitch count: 86 x 122

Stitched size (on 16-count Aida): 13.5 x 19cm (5⅜ x 7½in)

Stitch with two strands for cross stitch.

Essential supplies

- 1 skein of each DMC stranded cotton (floss) listed in the chart key

- 16-count Aida in Antique White, at least 34 x 39.5cm (13⅜ x 15½in)

MODEL STITCHED BY CLARE PROWSE

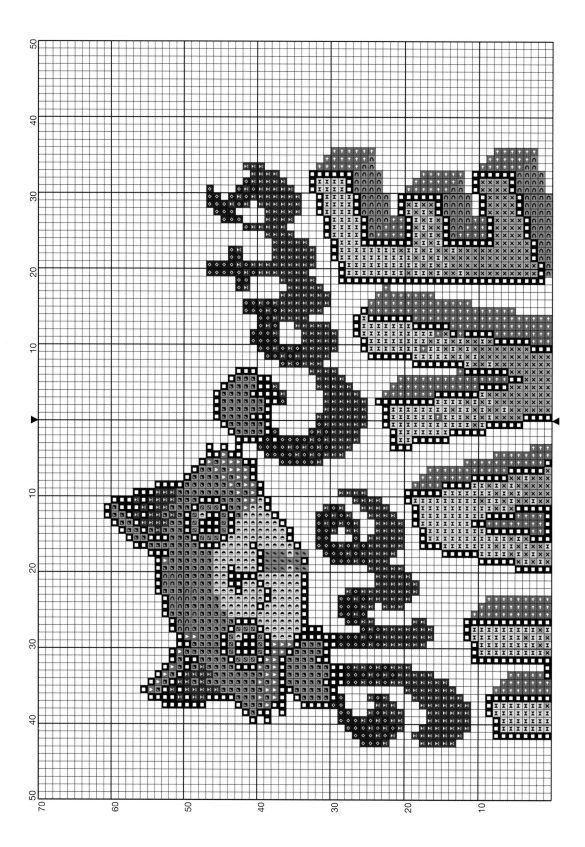

THREAD KEY

# 3	∩ 352	✕ 948	↑ 351	◢ 644	◨ 3819
✕ 350	◼ 598	◆ 3857	▶ 597	✕ 3326	✕ 3858
		◖ Ecru	□ 310		

63

*"*It's **ME**. It's always been **ME**. I mean there's no comparison, obviously. When you're on a **DiffeRent** plane of intelligence to the human male you know you'll always be **number one**.*"*

x

need to know

Stitch count: 120 x 158

Stitched size (on 16-count Aida): 19 x 25cm (7½ x 9⅞in)

Stitch with two strands for cross stitch.

Essential supplies

- 1 skein of each DMC stranded cotton (floss) listed in the chart key. If a colour requires more than one skein the number needed is indicated in brackets after the colour

- 16-count Aida in Antique White, at least 39.5 x 46cm (15½ x 18⅛in)

MODEL STITCHED BY
MADELEINE AYME-MCLEAN

THREAD KEY

< 168	◿ 413	⊢ 604	↓ 741	7 3771	◩ 3810	Z 169	6 444
⊠ 832	7 948	⊖ 3801	\ 307	◨ 498	⊔ 702	◈ 913	P 3708
N Ecru(2)	◪ 310(3)	+ 598	⊡ 704	↑ 3706	◣ Blanc		

Thread Key

| < 168 | ◢ 413 | ⊢ 604 | ↓ 741 | 7 3771 | ◩ 3810 | Z 169 | 6 444 | ⊠ 704 | 7 948 | ⊝ 3801 |
| \ 307 | ◱ 493 | ◳ 702 | ◈ 913 | P 3708 | N Ecru(2) | ◪ 310(3) | + 598 | ⊟ 910 | ↑ 3706 | ◣ Blanc |

69

"There's so much to be **donE** that the **humAns** seem to be blissfully unaware of: bag checking, plant pruning, bin sorting and toilet roll **unRolling** are just some of the tasks we will **assist** with."

X

Need to know

Stitch count: 124 x 172

Stitched size (on 14-count Aida): 22.5 x 31cm (8⅞ x 12¼in)

Stitch with three strands for cross stitch, and one strand for backstitch.

Essential supplies

- 1 skein of each DMC stranded cotton (floss) listed in the chart key. If a colour requires more than one skein the number needed is indicated in brackets after the colour

- 14-count Aida in Navy, at least 43 x 52cm (17 x 20½in)

MODEL STITCHED BY SUE MANSELL

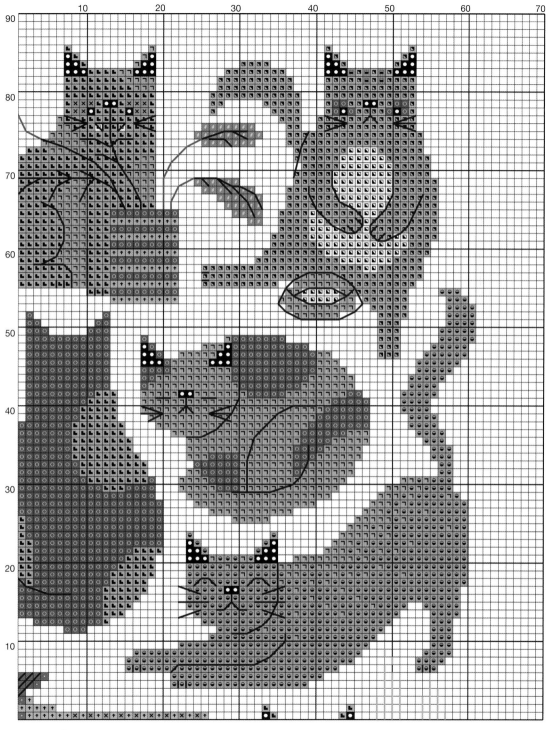

ThREAd KEY

O 310	# 704	▣ 3608	◪ 12	☒ 434	✚ 958	⊓ 3708(2)	↑ 747
▣ 436	◼ 964(2)	◎ 3839(2)	⊜ 3072	• 647	☒ 3341	◪ 3865	→ 3812

Backstitch

— 12 — 3865 —3812

— 3812 — 310 — 3072

73

THREAD KEY

⬤ 310	# 704	◼ 3608	◣ 12
☒ 434	✚ 958	⅂ 3708(2)	⬆ 747
◼ 436	◼ 964(2)	◎ 3839(2)	◓ 3072
• 647	✗ 3341	◣ 3865	➡ 3812

Backstitch

— 12 — 3865 — 3812
— 3812 — 310 — 3072

"We're **SELectiVE** in our taste. I personally single out pieces that I find **deeply** offensive, or positioned incorrectly. Ugly **vase** be gone. **TERRIBLE** tights, in the bin you go. It's a service we carry out for **FREE** and indefinitely."

x

Need to know

Stitch count: 86 x 121

Stitched size (on 14-count Aida): 15.5 x 22cm (6⅛ x 8⅝in)

Stitch with two strands for cross stitch.

Essential supplies

- 1 skein of each DMC stranded cotton (floss) listed in the chart key. If a colour requires more than one skein the number needed is indicated in brackets after the colour

- 14-count Aida in Pale Lemon, at least 35.5 x 42cm (14 x 16½in)

MODEL STITCHED BY KAYLEIGH WHITTON

I WILL

DESTROY

EVERYTHING ♥ YOU ♥ LOVE

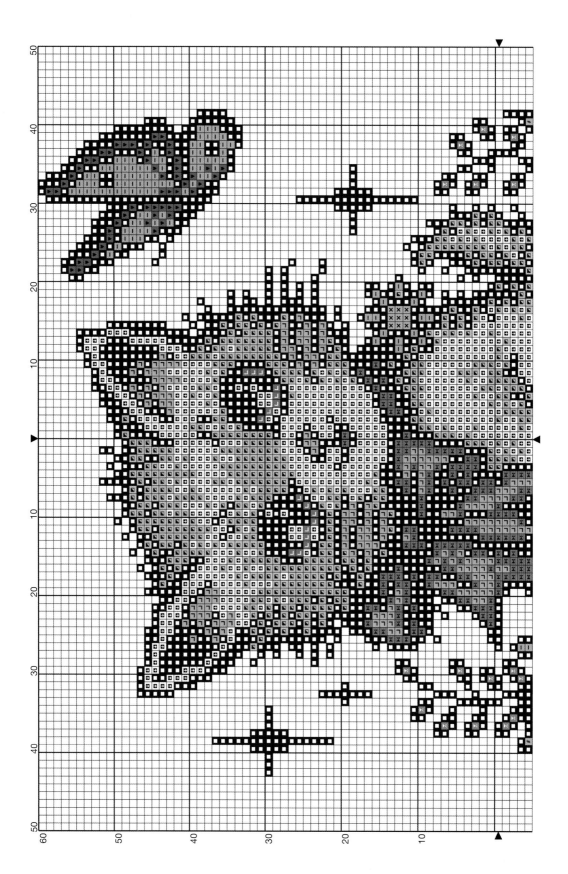

THREAD KEY

■ 25	⊠ 704	□ 310(2)	✗ 728
◆ 562	▐ 800	# 564	▶ 799
✗ 603	⌐ 3845	⌐ 605	⊡ Blanc

79

"We do **whAT** we want, when we want, like it or not. **HowLing** at the door in the middle of the night seems particularly **UNPOPULAR**... can't think why. We bring presents too, because who doesn't **LOVE** a dead bird?"

X

Need to know

Stitch count: 84 x 119

Stitched size (on 16-count Aida): 13.5 x 19cm (5⅜ x 7½in)

Stitch with two strands for cross stitch.

Essential supplies

- 1 skein of each DMC stranded cotton (floss) listed in the chart key. If a colour requires more than one skein the number needed is indicated in brackets after the colour

- 16-count Aida in Ice Blue, at least 33 x 39.5cm (13 x 15½in)

MODEL STITCHED BY EMMA RHODES

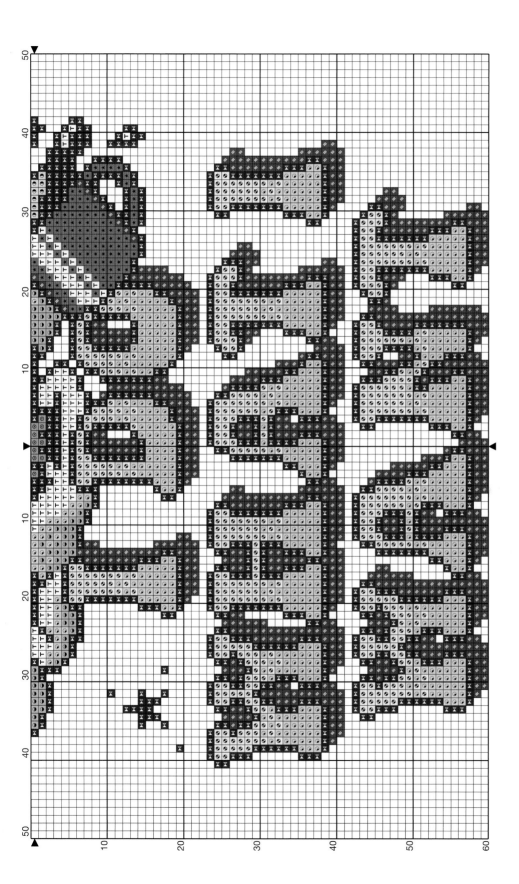

THREAD KEY

★	209	◑	3706
⊙	603	◈	3746
◐	727	T	Blanc
✕	333 (2)	◗	3708
◨	604	↓	3761
◉	818		

"Why are you Asleep at 04:15? This daily occurrence is becoming tiresomE. We have things to do! Why won't you set your human alarm? Now I have to do it with my beautiful voice. THank me later."

X

need to know

Stitch count: 86 x 120

Stitched size (on 16-count Aida): 13.5 x 19cm (5⅜ x 7½in)

Stitch with two strands for cross stitch.

Essential supplies

• 1 skein of each DMC stranded cotton (floss) listed in the chart key. If a colour requires more than one skein the number needed is indicated in brackets after the colour

• 16-count Aida in White, at least 34 x 39.5cm (13⅜ x 15½in)

MODEL STITCHED BY KIRSTY TORRANCE

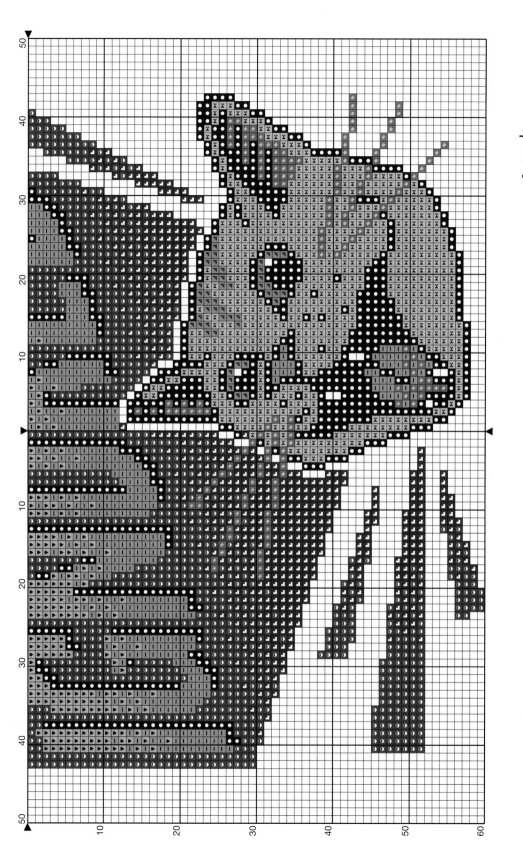

THREAD KEY

⊠	E980	●	310
◪	550	▮	741
◄	742	▨	3705
◑	3837 (2)	◤	3846

87

"We can tell a **trUE** cat person - they'll always be part of our family - lots of humans **SUCK** after all. It's true that she talks to us a **LOT**, so It's good we hate the same things. We also keep secrets in **exchangE** for food, etc."

x

need to know

Stitch count: 121 x 171

Stitched size (on 14-count Aida): 22 x 31cm (8⅝ x 12¼in)

Stitch with two strands for cross stitch.

Essential supplies

- 1 skein of each DMC stranded cotton (floss) listed in the chart key. If a colour requires more than one skein the number needed is indicated in brackets after the colour

- 14-count Aida in Cream, at least 42 x 51cm (16½ x 20in)

MODEL STITCHED BY SHARON ATKINSON

THREAD KEY

🗡 3766	Ⓩ 3839	
◐ 310(3)	◢ 604	
↑ 3824	◣ 152	
◑ 603	◤ 3340	
🗡 18	✛ 225	

"*Observe* this day in the life of **ME**. Aren't I **GREAt?** Look at me doing all the things. What? **Meow** to you too!"

need to know

Stitch count: 170 x 121

Stitched size (on 16-count Aida): 27 x 19cm (10⅝ x 7½in)

Stitch with two strands for cross stitch, and one strand for backstitch.

Essential supplies

- 1 skein of each DMC stranded cotton (floss) listed in the chart key. If a colour requires more than one skein the number needed is indicated in brackets after the colour

- 16-count Aida in Black, at least 47 x 39.5cm (18½ x 15½in)

MODEL STITCHED BY ELAINA FRIEND

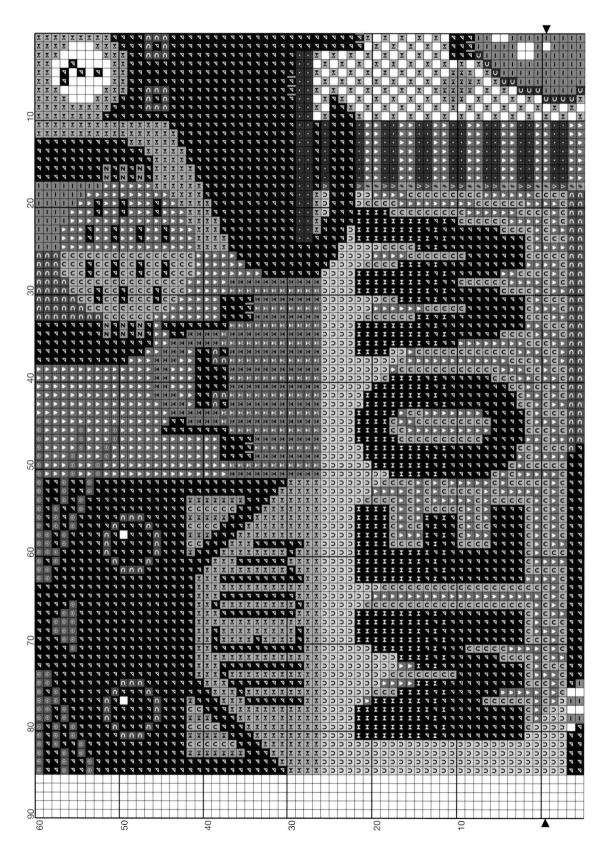

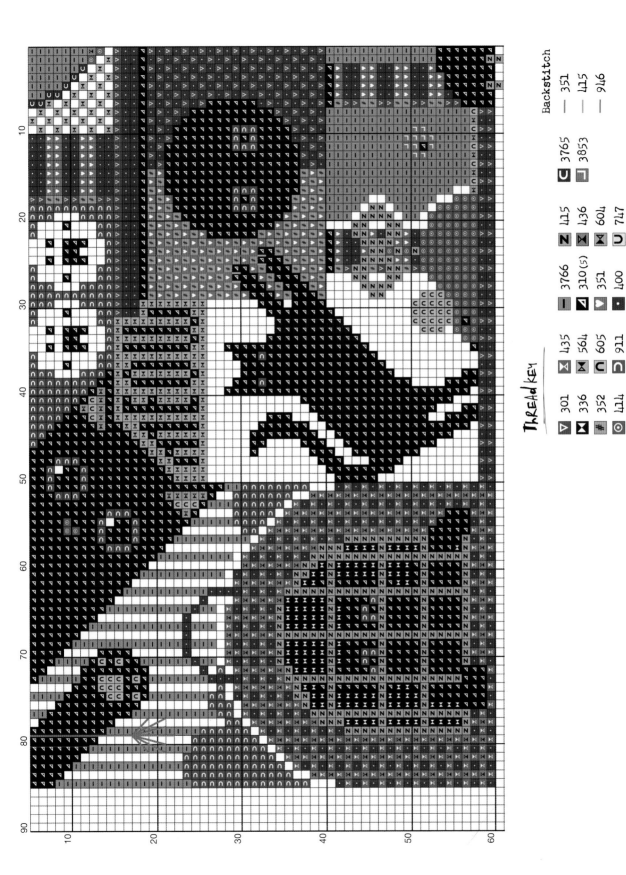

Backstitch
— 351
— 415
— 946

Thread Key		
▷ 301	✕ 435	☒ 3766
✕ 336	☒ 564	◤ 310(5)
# 352	⊂ 605	▶ 351
⊙ 414	∩ 911	■ 400
⊍ 3765	N 415	
⊓ 3853	✕ 436	
	☒ 604	
	⊍ 747	

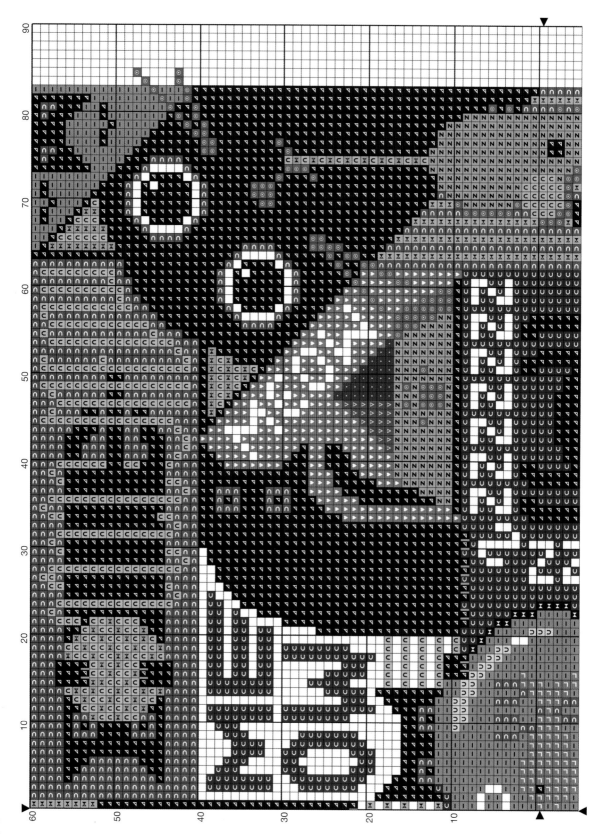

Backstitch
— 351
— 415
— 946

U 3765	**C** 3765	
T 3853		

N 415	**X** 436	**X** 604	**U** 747

I 3766	**◣** 310(5)	**▶** 351	**▪** 400

THREAD KEY

▷ 301	**X** 435	**C** 564	**∩** 605
X 336	**X** 352	**#** 414	**◎** 911

"Some **humans** are obsessed with us... which is **understandaBLE.** We'll come out for the occasional meow if we see you. Stroking is **stRiCTLy** on our terms though."

X

need to know

Stitch count: 87 x 123

Stitched size (on 16-count Aida): 14 x 19.5cm (5½ x 7¾in)

Stitch with two strands for cross stitch, and one strand for backstitch.

Essential supplies

- 1 skein of each DMC stranded cotton (floss) listed in the chart key

- 16-count Aida in Black, at least 34 x 39.5cm (13⅜ x 15½in)

MODEL STITCHED BY CAROLINE GRAYLING

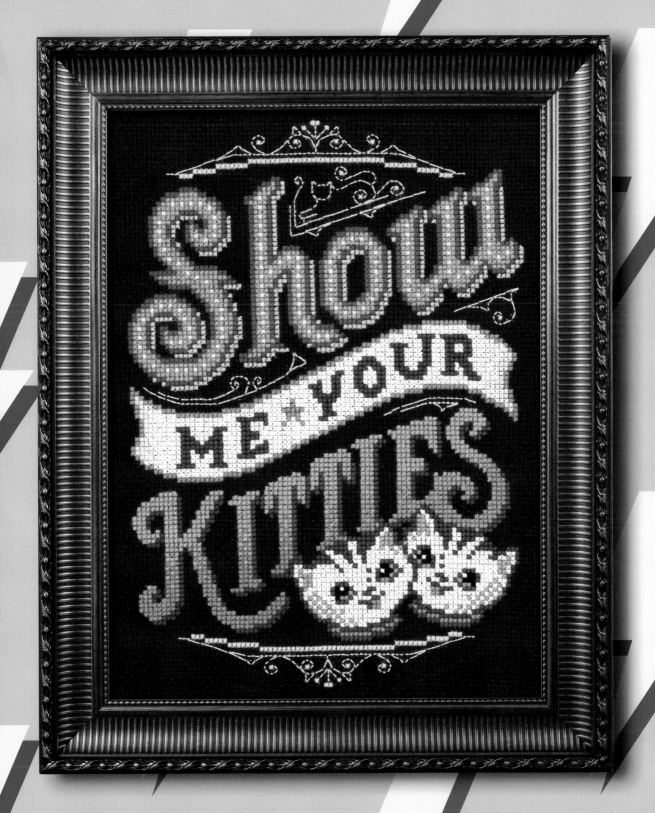

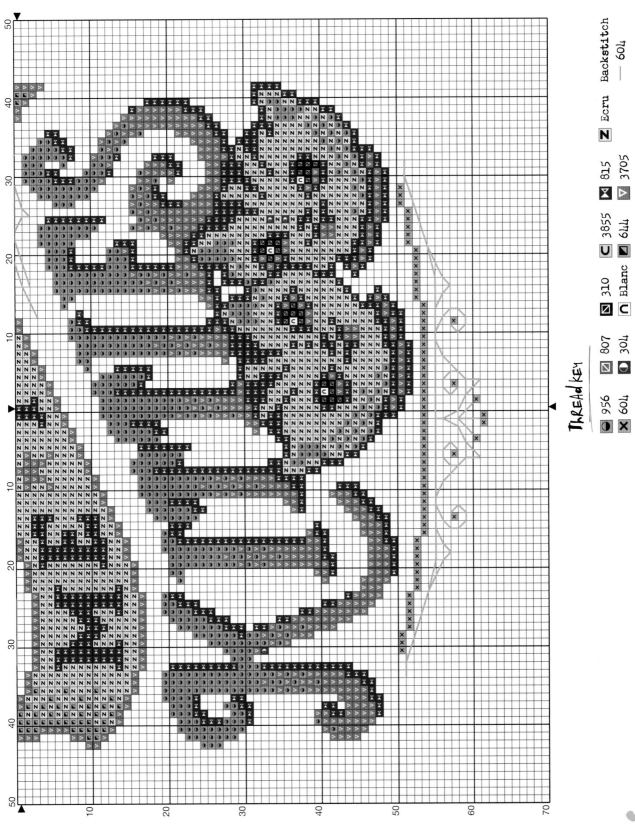

THREAD KEY

◐ 956	☑ 807	**◯** 304
✕ 604	U 3855	Z 310
	✕ 644	C Blanc
	✕ 815	N Ecru
	▷ 3705	

Backstitch
— 604

TECHNIQUES

PREPARING THE FABRIC

Always begin by ensuring that you have a piece of fabric that's large enough for your design (and relatively free of cat hair). Make sure there is a good amount of clearance around the edge to allow for framing – I recommend at least 10cm (4in) on each side. To find the centre of the Aida fabric, fold the fabric in half and then in half again. Mark the centre point with a needle.

It's rubbish getting halfway through a piece and realizing the edges of your fabric are getting all frayed and tatty. A good way to avoid this is to use a zigzag stitch on a sewing machine to keep your edges tidy. If you don't have a sewing machine, fear not! Masking tape folded over all of the sides is an easy alternative. Just remember to add a little extra fabric to the area if you plan to do this, as you will need to chop it off before washing.

NOTE: Stitching onto black fabric can be tricky. For some larger or more complicated designs I prefer to use a wider weave fabric such as 14-count Aida so I can see the holes in the weave more clearly. In these instances I stitch 3-ply (with three strands rather than my usual two), so that I still get really good coverage with fewer visible gaps.

CROSS STITCH

Once you've got the hang of this, the rest is a doddle! Working with two strands of thread in your needle (or three if working on some dark fabrics, see note), start your first cross stitch in the centre of the design and the centre of your fabric. You can stitch in rows by colour or individually depending on your preference (I tend to mix and match, depending on how I'm feeling).

To start, bring the needle up through the back of the fabric, leaving a 2cm (1in) tail of thread behind, which you should secure with your subsequent stitches. Take the needle back down through the fabric, creating a diagonal stitch, making sure that the thread tail at the back stays in place. Keep doing this until you have finished a row (1), and then come back the other way, crossing the stitches diagonally to complete the row (2). Try to keep all the top stitches running in the same direction, as it creates a neater finish.

Continue to stitch until you have finished a section in that colour. At the end of the last cross stitch, the needle should be at the back of the fabric. Thread the needle through the back of four or five stitches to secure the thread, then cut away any excess.

Making a row of cross stitch on Aida

Making a row of cross stitch on linen

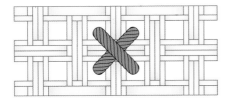
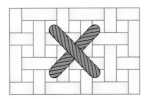

Completed cross stitch on Aida

Completed cross stitch on linen

BACKSTITCH

This stitch is ideal for adding detail, but it can be less forgiving than cross stitch. For backstitch, you should use a single strand of thread.

To start, bring the needle up through the fabric at the point of the first stitch, leaving a 2cm (1in) tail at the back, which you should secure with your subsequent stitches. Bring the needle back through the fabric at the point where the stitch will finish to create one backstitch. Next, bring the needle up at the point where the next stitch will finish and back down through the point where the first stitch starts. Continue until all of the backstitches in the chosen area have been completed.

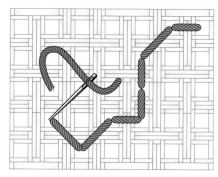

Backstitch on Aida

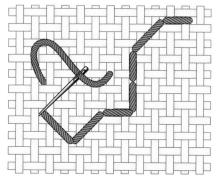

Backstitch on linen

STITCH COUNT AND DESIGN SIZE

For each design in this book I have given the finished size and stitch count based on the type of fabric and size of weave that I have used. It is important to note that if you choose an alternative count of fabric it will change the finished design size.

To work out the size of your final design, first check the stitch count, which is given under Need to Know on each project. Each number should then be divided by the count of the fabric you're using in order to give you the width and height in inches.

For Aida fabric the count represents the number of threads per inch. For linen it's the same but, because you stitch over two threads rather than one, divide the count by two before making your calculations.

For example, if the finished size of the design is given as 120 w x 140 h on 16-count fabric (or 32-count linen):

120 divided by 16 = 7½in

140 divided by 16 = 8¾in

The final design size is 7½ x 8¾in (or 19 x 22.25cm)

There are plenty of calculators available online if your brain feels like it has turned to mush at this point! Or you can ask your cat to help – but don't expect them to share their mathematical genius. They save that up for calculating the trajectory required to land on the bird table.

FOLLOWING CHARTS

Charts are made up of multiple coloured squares, each featuring symbols, which refer to a chart key. Here's a handy guide:

- Each coloured square represents a whole cross stitch.

- The symbols relate to specific thread colours in each chart and should be cross-referenced against the key next to that chart.

- Single lines of colour represent backstitches, and the thread colour for these is also given in the key.

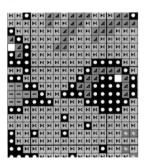

THREAD KEY

Symbol	Colour	Symbol	Colour
⋈	E980	◯	310
⬛	550	▬	741
♥	742	⬙	3705
◓	3837 (2)	◢	3846

CLEANING

Always hand wash your work with a delicate detergent in warm water. Do not rub or wring, but rather soak and gently agitate after a few minutes. Rinse well in cold water and allow to dry flat. This should remove all unwanted paw prints. I'm always terrified to wash pieces, but as long as you've used good quality, branded stranded cotton and colourfast fabric you should have no issues with colours running. When you're ready to iron, place a towel on your ironing board and then iron your piece right side down over this, using a hot steam setting. *Et voila!*

FRAMING

There are so many options for framing embroidery these days, so feel free to choose what works for you. I sometimes just use a simple hoop, which is laced from the back. This inexpensive method of framing is perfect for creating multiple designs for a feature wall. You can also paint the hoops or wrap them with ribbon for added pops of complementary colour.

Throughout this book I have used a few different framing options to demonstrate the various effects you can create. Take a look through the pages and choose your favourite – you may decide to replicate the method I've chosen for a particular design or to try something new.

CONVERSION CHART

I have used DMC thread; however, if you prefer, you can use Anchor, which is just as good. This conversion chart shows all the colours used in this book.

DMC	Anchor	DMC	Anchor	DMC	Anchor	DMC	Anchor	DMC	Anchor
1	1037	340	118	702	226	921	1003	3801	1098
2	234	350	11	704	256	932	1033	3805	62
3	398	351	10	721	925	946	332	3806	62
4	235	352	9	727	293	948	1011	3810	1066
12	253	355	1014	728	305	956	40	3812	188
14	1043	400	351	729	890	958	187	3819	253
16	1043	413	236	741	304	959	186	3820	306
17	278	414	235	742	303	963	73	3821	305
18	295	415	398	744	301	964	185	3822	295
19	305	434	310	747	158	977	1002	3823	386
25	103	435	1046	783	306	980 (E980*)	278	3824	8
33	92	436	1045	797	132	996	433	3825	323
151	73	437	362	799	136	3072	847	3826	1049
152	969	444	290	800	144	3326	36	3837	100
155	1030	498	1005	807	168	3340	329	3838	177
161	176	550	101	813	161	3341	328	3839	176
165	278	562	210	815	43	3607	87	3845	1089
168 (E168*)	234	564	206	818	23	3608	86	3846	1090
169	849	597	1064	826	161	3705	35	3847	1076
209	109	598	1062	829	906	3706	33	3853	1003
225	1026	602	57	831	277	3708	31	3855	311
301	1049	603	62	832	907	3731	76	3857	936
304	1006	604	55	833	907	3746	1030	3858	1007
307	289	605	1094	894	27	3752	1032	3865	2
310	403	606	334	904	258	3761	928	Blanc	2
311	148	613	831	906	256	3765	170	Ecru	387
319	218	644	830	911	205	3766	167		
333	119	647	1040	912	209	3771	336		
336	150	676	891	913	204	3799	236		

* DMC Light Effects E168 and E980 can be substituted for regular DMC floss if preferred. There is no metallic colour match available for either in Anchor, so please use 234 for E168 and 278 for E980 if converting.

ABOUT THE AUTHOR

Emma Congdon studied Graphic Design at the University of the Arts, London. She worked as a graphic designer for advertising and design agencies for many years before rediscovering her love of cross stitch and becoming a freelance designer in order to pursue this passion. Her design work regularly features in magazines such as *Cross Stitcher*, *Cross Stitch Crazy* and *World of Cross Stitching*, and she has designed several pieces for DMC. This is her fourth book, and follows the success of her previous publications, *Cross Stitch for the Soul*, *Cross Stitch for the Earth* and *Cross Stitch for the Heart*. Emma has two cats (but will probably end up with more).

ACKNOWLEDGEMENTS

Many thanks for all the hard work put in by everyone at David and Charles in the making of this book. In particular Ame Verso for commissioning the idea, as well as designers Anna Wade and Prudence Rogers for such beautiful layouts. Thanks to Jane Trollope, my editor, for all of her attention to detail, and ability to make sense of my waffle. To the stitchers involved in creating the models, Sharon Atkinson, Eleanor Cooper, Glenda Dickson, Hayley Wellock, Madeleine Ayme-McLean, Kayleigh Whitton, Emma Rhodes, Kirsty Torrance, Clare Prowse, Sue Mansell, Caroline Grayling and Elaina Friend, thank you so much, you've done a sterling job and I could not be prouder. Jason Jenkins, thank you for photographing them all so wonderfully too. Thank you to my family for your love and support as always, and last but not least (the most important of all) my dastardly cats Oscar and Teddy, and my rainbow cat George, for all their 'help' in creating this book.

STITCHERS

All the model stitchers have been mentioned in the projects. The cover image was stitched by Eleanor Cooper.

INDEX

Printed in China through Asia Pacific Offset for:
David and Charles, Ltd
Suite A, Tourism House, Pynes Hill, Exeter, EX2 5WS

10 9 8 7 6 5 4 3 2 1

Publishing Director: Ame Verso
Managing Editor: Jeni Chown
Editor: Jessica Cropper
Project Editor: Jane Trollope
Head of Design: Anna Wade
Designer: Prudence Rogers
Pre-press Designer: Ali Stark
Photography: Jason Jenkins
Production Manager: Beverley Richardson

David and Charles publishes high-quality books on a wide range of subjects.
For more information visit www.davidandcharles.com.

Share your makes with us on social media using #dandcbooks and follow us
on Facebook and Instagram by searching for @dandcbooks.

Layout of the digital edition of this book may vary depending on reader hardware and display settings.